Tales of Healing

Tales of Healing

*Stories of those who came to Jesus
for healing and who found their
lives profoundly changed*

Rosi Morgan-Barry

Kingdom Publishers

Tales of Healing

Copyright© Rosi Morgan – Barry

All rights reserved. No part of this book may be reproduced in any form by photocopying or any electronic or mechanical means, including information storage or retrieval systems, without permission in writing from both the copyright owner and the publisher of the book. The right of to be identified as the author of this work has been asserted by her in accordance with the Copyright, Designs and Patents Act 1988 and any subsequent amendments thereto. A catalogue record for this book is available from the British Library.

All Scripture Quotations have been taken from the New English Bible

ISBN: 978-1-911697-57-2

1st Edition by Kingdom Publishers, London, UK.

You can purchase copies of this book from any leading bookstore or email contact@kingdompublishers.co.uk

"That evening, after sunset, they brought to him all who were ill, or possessed by devils, and the whole town was there, gathered at the door. He healed many who suffered from various diseases, and drove out many devils. He would not let the devils speak, because they knew who he was."

(Mark 1: 32 – 34, NEB)

Table of Contents

Devil spirit: *Mark 1: 23 – 28*	3
Live to serve: *Mark 1: 29 – 31*	7
Don't tell: *Mark 1: 40 – 45*	11
Guilty conscience: *Mark 2: 2 – 12*	15
Useless limb: *Mark 3: 1 – 6*	21
Deathly sleep: *Mark 5: 21 – 24, 35 – 43*	25
Secret problem: *Mark 5: 25 – 34*	29
A foreigner's faith: *Mark 7: 24 – 30*	33
Speech Therapy: *Mark 7: 31 – 37*	37
Blind Cure: *Mark 8: 22 – 26*	41
Despair to hope: *Mark 9: 14 – 24*	45
Shout aloud: *Mark 10: 46 – 52*	49

In the gospels we read of folk who came, or were brought to Jesus for healing, and who found their lives profoundly changed.

What had their lives been up to the moment of healing?

How many of them went on to do what illness, paralysis or disease had once prevented?

How many were able to find a new way of living?

How many of them simply went back to what they had once been, to what they had once done?

There are very few clues in the Bible stories which answer these questions; they are answers we shall never know, but can perhaps imagine.

These stories from Mark's gospel explore what life may have been like for those suffering from diseases which were common at the time, and what happened to those who experienced the Lord's miraculous healing.

The tales, taken from Mark's gospel, may provide life lessons for us all – especially those whose work is within the healing professions, and who have to make life or death choices that few of us would want to face.

***

Devil spirit

Mark 1: 23 – 28

'There was in the synagogue a man in the grip of an unclean spirit ...'

What can I tell you of my life? There was a time before, and a time before that and there is the time after both, which is now. I would rather tell of the now of my life, but you have asked of the times before and before and I need to tell you of them, and of the great upheaval between them, which took no time at all.

To begin with the first of times: memory is dim here, but it was my childhood time, and a happy time. I was the first in my family, and my mother and father seemed pleased to have me as their child. At least at first. My father was a potter who made good pots, and had a stall in the market place; my mother was kind and beautiful. But as I grew, she faded. Life for her seemed to be an uncertain thing. She did was what was needed for my father and me: such as preparing food, drawing water from the well, providing clean clothes, but seemed to hover between these everyday tasks and a strangeness of spirit which took her into herself and away from us. At those times, there was something of fear in her. When my sister was born, the child took all our mother's spirit and with it, her life.

But I loved my baby sister, my mother in miniature, and I began to understand my mother's fading of spirit, her uncertainties, as I had them too. Things of everyday became shadowy, and instead there was in my head another Thing, which seemed to share my body. This Thing would sometimes shout out words I did not know I had in my head and often did not understand.

After some years, I went away; which became the time before. I lived alone in the hills and caves with this strange spirit inside my head which was my evil companion. My sister brought me food, and would often stay and talk quietly with me when the demon was silent. But if I began to rave and shout, she would slip away.

One day she came with an air of excitement. She gave me the food and as I ate, she told me of a new teacher. One like no other she said. His words stirred peoples' souls and and made them think new thoughts. I laughed; I remembered the teaching in synagogue school from the scribes, which took us round in circles: saying this great Rabbi said this, but that great Rabbi said that, and another one said something else. My sister interrupted me; this man was not like that, she said. It was as if he knew God's very words and spoke them clearly. He taught out on the hillside, not just in the synagogue on the Sabbath, and anyone could go and listen to him.

'Perhaps', my sister said wistfully, 'you could come and hear him too'.

That made me laugh again and the demon woke and laughed, cackling with scorn and derision.

But after much thought I did go. One Sabbath, I crept into the synagogue.

He was there, the man Jesus. At once, my demon began to rave and shout, words I did not know and did not understand.

'Hey, you! Yes, you! Jesus of Nazareth! What have we to do with you? Ha! Have you come to destroy us? I know you! You're God's Holy One!' and he went into his cackles of strange laughter.

I felt myself being shaken and my mouth and eyes were wet. Everyone in the synagogue was silent, looking at me, some with horror, some with pity, the scribes with scorn, signalling to the leader to grab me and throw me out.

But then the man Jesus spoke. Quietly and firmly.

'Be silent! Come out! Leave him alone. Now!'

I heard myself scream loudly and felt myself being flung down. And then – silence.

That was all. Jesus helped me up for I felt as weak as a child, and my sister came flying down from the women's gallery and ran to me. My father came too and we all walked together out of the synagogue, through a hum of questions and comments, through subdued laughter and astonishment.

That was the time between the before and the now. I am happy in the now of my life and I can tell without shame of the before time. I work with my father, but my true work is to tell the story of my meeting with the teacher and healer called Jesus.

The man who gave me new hope, new joy, new life.

***

Live to serve

Mark 1: 29 – 31

'Simon's mother-in-law was sick in bed with a fever ...'

'Old age,' my mother used to say, 'is not for the faint-hearted!'

Of course I laughed. My mother did not seem old to me then; she was always busy, always working, often laughing. She would tell us children funny stories; things she remembered from her own childhood; things she heard in the market-place, tales told at the well. She was

the strength and stay of our house. But of course that was all a long time ago, and I am as old now as she was when she made that remark. Now of course, I know what she meant.

Something else my mother used to say, especially when things were difficult, was simply:

'Don't fret, don't worry, just get on with it!'

By which she meant stop moaning or complaining, just carry on with life and work.

So, I just carried on through good times and bad times, until now – the now of being old. My daughter is married to the fisherman Simon – a good man, but inclined to put his mouth where his head ought to be. When my husband died and I became a widow, which was one of the worst of times, Simon took me into his home and made me welcome. I was glad to be able to help with the tasks of the household: cleaning, washing, making bread, cooking, fetching water, taking baskets of fish to the market. Then when the babies came, helping with them when tiny, and later, teaching my grand-daughters and listening to the boys recite their lessons. My daughter says she could not do without me. So I try to be useful. If I cannot be useful, what am I still here for? So I did what all women do, and did it gladly.

Until the day – it was a Sabbath – when the burning fever came, suddenly. I had got up as usual, began such chores as were permitted on the Sabbath, but began to feel as though the room was moving around me, as though the inside of my head was moving. One moment I was preparing the Sabbath meal, the next I could hardly walk, could not even stand upright, and took to my bed, my head bursting with pain. As the fever spread over my body, I could not bear the feel of the cloth covering me. My daughter talked anxiously of getting the priest to come. She told me he could carry out a ritual with an iron knife tied with hair to a thorn bush, and then recite the scriptures – the story of the burning bush which was not burnt, and God being in the fire. How that was supposed to help I do not know. But this ritual, together with a certain bit of some sort of magic formula was supposed to be the cure for the fever. She waited in anxiety for Simon to come back from the synagogue so that she could ask him about it.

He did come, and brought that new Rabbi, Jesus, the one who had stirred their hearts and minds with his teachings. I had heard them talking about him as I helped serve the evening meal. So now he was here. My daughter, ever conscious of the duty of hospitality, was nonetheless put out, but did her best not to show it. I was too ill to be of any use, and Simon and Andrew had brought three guests: James and John and this man Jesus!

Apparently, so I heard later, Simon in his usual blunt way told him – Jesus – about my sickness. As soon as he knew what had happened to me he came to see me. His eyes were kind. He did not say anything, did not ask for a knife or bit of hair; he did not mutter a bit of scripture or recite any kind of magic spell. He just took hold of my hand and held it. His hand was cool and suddenly that feeling of coolness spread from his hand to mine. From his touch, the burning pain ebbed away and was gone. Then he simply helped me get up.

So I did. I got up – and, well, just got on with it.

Did I thank him properly? I can't remember, there were things to do to bring in the Sabbath: lighting the candles, serving the food.

But I will always remember his quiet kindliness, the cool touch of his hand. And I will never forget that he gave me back my usefulness.

I can go on being useful.

I can live to serve.

***

Don't tell

Mark 1: 40 – 45

'A man suffering from a dreaded skin disease came to Jesus …'

'Don't tell', he said, 'don't say anything. Do what the Law says: let the priest examine you.'

How did he think I could get away with that? There would be questions asked, hard questions, and if I refused to answer them, people would make up their own minds, write their own narrative. So I told a few of those who had known me as a careless boy, and a thoughtless young man. Those who knew too of the time when the rash started.

I didn't take much notice of it at first. Just a small, white itchy spot at the base of my thumb. Then another popped up and my father panicked. Packed me off to the priest.

No need for the priest to tell me what I thought I knew. Once the scaly outbreaks could be seen on my face and arms, I was told I had to leave home and family. I was told not to enter the synagogue, not to go to the market or join any crowd of people. I was not allowed to wash myself or my clothes in stream or river where others might draw water. I must not go out without my torn shirt and must always have my head bare. I must always cry out 'unclean!' if anyone came near me. There was no hope for me. I did as I was told.

I roamed the hills, and took shelter in a small cave. My mother brought a bit of food for me each day, and sometimes she would sit on a stone outside the cave and tell me the news of the market-place. One day she told me about the strange new teacher who had healed all kinds of diseases. He even drove out demons, she said. Then she was silent a minute.

'Might heal you', she added, then got up and went away.

I thought and thought. *'Might heal you'*, she'd said. Would he? But why would he? But if he healed others, why not me? My thoughts went round in circles. I just had to believe he could. I'll do it, I suddenly decided. Go and find this man Jesus and ask him. But then, I thought, that would be breaking the law, I had no right to go and speak to him, I was not allowed to enter the town. Perhaps better to stay a leper. Always? For the rest of my life? Suddenly I knew I was being offered the chance to be well, to be clean, to do something useful with my life instead of staying as I was.

I got up – and went.

I remembered when I had gone to see the priest and been told to see no-one, but to reflect on the sin, which had caused the disease, and to repent. I did reflect, on my life, my disease and the sin. But what was that sin? How could I repent of something I didn't know I had done?

But now, I *knew* I was committing a sin: that of approaching Jesus, and asking if he could heal me. *That* was forbidden. I should have carried the burden of my leprous body to my grave, avoiding all contact with anyone. But when my mother told me Jesus of Nazareth was in Galilee, what did I do? Forgot about all those forbidden things, and went searching through the hills and villages for him. When I found him, I went straight up to him, knelt and begged him to heal me, as I knew he could.

I knew too he would not turn away as others did; would not rage at me for daring to approach him, would not regard me with disgust, as others did. How did I know these things? I don't know. But I was right. Not only did he *not* turn away, he stretched out his hand and took hold of mine.

'Of course I want to,' he said. 'Be clean!'

He pulled me to my feet.

I looked down at my once dirty, scaly, disease-ridden body and saw clean, fresh skin. I looked *clean,* felt *clean.* I wanted to run and jump and shout: *'I'm clean!'*

But that was when he said I must not tell anyone but do what the Law said. So I did. Collected the birds, the lamb, the oil, went and offered the sacrifice. Went home and washed and waited. After the seven days went back and was given the certificate to say 'officially clean'. Went out to begin my life again. With joy.

I knew then what I wanted to do with the rest of my life. I wanted to make for lepers such as I had been, a quiet, sheltering place; a place where they could rest, where they need not be hounded from town to town, where they could perhaps find some peace of mind, perhaps even healing of body.

I wanted to give to others some small part of what had been given to me.

***

Guilty conscience

Mark 2: 2 – 12

'Jesus was preaching the message to them, when four men arrived, carrying a paralysed man ...'

My word! If there is anyone in the world who ought to give thanks for faithful friends, for an amazing healer, for newness of life, then that one is my friend Joses. If there is anyone who must turn his life around, then he is the one. But does he look back on what he once was? I'm not sure. Lives for the moment, does Jo. For him, the past is a forgotten place; the future does not exist. For him, there is only the now, and that to be enjoyed to the full. But that was before. Maybe now, he stops and thinks – just a little.

There were five of us, born in Capernaum within weeks of each other, going to synagogue school together, playing together and getting up to all kinds of mischief. Our mothers would meet at the well and shake their heads over us, but as my mother used to say: get one of those boys on his own and he was quite manageable; it was only once we were together that the mischief started. And it was nearly always Jo who started it!

But of course we grew up. Had good behaviour beaten into us, learned the Commandments and the Law, and the lessons of everyday life, such as: 'no work, no food'. Found work, wives, homes, families. Well, four of us did, and settled down. Guess who was the odd one out? Jo of course.

But he found work: lots of work of different kinds, but couldn't settle to anything for any length of time. Helped on his father's farm, then tried woodwork, building work, leather-work, and was handy at all of them. But settle down? That he could not – would not do. Neither could he seem to find the right girl to settle down with; he still hankered after childish exploits and mischief. His main interest was enjoying himself with games: wrestling or boxing, both of which he loved and usually managed to win.

It was after one of his boxing bouts that things went wrong for him. He'd been persuaded to take on a man much bigger than himself and although Jo, light and quick on his feet as he was, managed to avoid being hit too often, he was finally knocked down by his opponent. He struggled to his feet and limped away, to the jeers of the crowd. He was angry, blazingly angry, and went off by himself.

We didn't see him for a day or two. Then I heard the man who'd floored Jo had been found beaten up. Badly injured too. Of course we all immediately thought of Jo and went in search of him, only to find he had taken to his bed, completely unable to move. That last blow he'd received had, it seemed, been more serious than we thought.

We took it in turns to visit him, take him the news, tell him what was happening in Capernaum, trying to get him interested in what was going on. But he was completely apathetic, not interested in anything. It was hard to see him like this, with all the life knocked out of him. I think I was the one who told him about Jesus the healer, and we all agreed that, if we could get him to see this Jesus, he might be able to help him.

We put our minds to it, came up with the idea of carrying him on a mat and asking the healer to do something for poor Jo. We rigged up a stretcher, tied Jo on to it, and jogged through the streets, trying not to tip Jo off, until we came to the house. But then met a problem. A huge crowd had jammed the pavement outside the door and no-one was prepared to give way to us with our burden. Not sure which one of us suggested the roof, but we latched onto the idea and hoisted the mat, with Jo clinging to it, up the outside stair. We could hear Jesus telling a story in the room below. We dug out the brushwood between the beams and gently lowered Jo, still clinging to his mat, right down to Jesus' feet. Then we lay on our bellies and peered down to see what would happen next.

There were gasps of astonishment and some laughter, and then we heard Jesus say:

'My son, your sins are forgiven'.

What on earth did he mean by that? How could he forgive sins? How could he know what Jo may, or may not have done? How could saying that make Jo better? We weren't the only ones puzzling over his words; there were some scribes sitting there in front of everyone else and we could hear them muttering among themselves. Then Jesus said:

'Why are you thinking such thoughts? What's easier: to tell this poor man his sins are forgiven or to tell him to get up and walk? Anyone can simply say 'Get up and walk' but can anyone prove his authority to offer forgiveness for the sin that caused this man to lie helpless here?'

No-one answered that; not one of those scribes, clever in matters of the Law as they were, could find an answer. So Jesus answered his own question. He turned to Jo.

'Get up my son! Pick up your mat, and walk home!'

There was a pause. Then Jo did exactly that. When we carried him into the house, he'd hardly been able to lift a finger; now he slowly got up, bent and picked up the mat and walked through the crowd which parted in awe to let him go.

We all came clattering down the outside stairs, laughing and shouting, clapping him on the back, asking how he felt. Jo laughed and joked with the rest of us. It was like having our old Jo back again.

In the weeks that followed, Jo was very much his old self: playful, funny, careless, just as he used to be. Trying to settle to work but doing something one week and something else the next. Joking with girls of doubtful repute, getting up to mischief. It was as though his paralysis had never happened.

Yet, there were moments when he was quiet, reflective. One of these occurred not long after his healing, when we were all my house. My wife, astonished but delighted at seeing Jo well again, had made us welcome and prepared an evening meal for us. Sitting round the fire that evening, Jo began to tell how he felt, what he understood to have happened to him.

'After that fight,' he said, 'I couldn't think of anything other than getting my own back on the man who'd beaten me. Yes, I know it was a fair fight, but I wanted revenge. So I went and found him, laughing and boasting about what he'd done to me, and I just pulled him out and gave him a good hiding. And that *wasn't* a fair fight, he was unprepared and a bit drunk. I felt really bad about that. Felt guilty. Next day, I woke stiff and bruised and found I couldn't move. You all know the rest.'

We were silent. Yes, of course we knew, we'd been there. Seen it happen. But did we truly

understand?

Did we know who it was who had healed Jo?

Put very simply: the man Jesus said Jo's sins were forgiven, and it was the sin that made him weak and helpless. But the priests say only God can forgive sins.

Jesus then proved that Jo was forgiven because he healed him.

What did that mean? Who was this man?

Where did his power come from?

One day I thought, we might know the answers.

Even Jo.

***

Useless limb

Mark 3: 1 – 6

> ... *'in the synagogue, there was a man who had a paralysed hand.'*

The Law is quite definite on this point – as indeed on many points. As a Teacher of the Law, I know what it says, and what it means. I know the answers to the many questions about how a good son of Abraham should live and how he should keep the Law. Especially I know the Law as applied to the Sabbath Day, with the apparently simple commandment:

'Observe the Sabbath and keep it holy. You have six days in which to do your work but the seventh day is a day of rest dedicated to God. On that day, no-one is to work ...'

We who know the Law also know answers to the questions about what is 'work' and how should it be defined in the light of what is necessary to maintain life. I have taught many boys, some of whom come up with cheeky questions about what it is permitted to do on the Sabbath, such as:

'If I drop my breakfast bread-roll, am I allowed to pick it up?' That question I ignored.

Or: 'If I cut my finger on the Sabbath, can I put a bandage on it?'

That was indeed a more serious question and I told the child that although to heal is to work, simple measures might be taken to help someone in need of healing. He could indeed put a bandage on a cut finger, but he must not apply any ointment. An injury could be prevented from getting worse, but it could not be made better.

But this man Jesus, who had by all accounts been to Rabbinic school, did not seem to have learnt the simplest lessons of the Law. That is what I thought then – now I am not so sure.

What put the doubts and uncertainties into my mind? One particular incident.

I was one of a deputation from the Sanhedrin to attend Sabbath worship in Capernaum. We had been told to keep an eye on the words and works of this man Jesus; he had been suspected of breaking the Sabbath on more than one occasion and we were there, in the seats of honour, to ensure he, or indeed any-one, did not mislead people with either words or deeds.

He was there. His disciples were gathered about him. So too was a man, a stone mason by trade, whose right hand was withered and useless. Probably from some carelessness in his work I thought. We all watched the man Jesus. What would he do? It was a situation he would exploit to his advantage, no doubt.

He called the man to the front. Then he turned and looking straight at us – the Sanhedrin deputation – and asked three simple questions:

'What does our Law allow us to do on the Sabbath? To help or to harm? To save a life or destroy it?'

The answers, I thought then, were obvious. To help, certainly, but what help does this man need? To save a life of course, but his life was not in danger. He could perfectly well wait until the end of Sabbath to be healed.

Jesus apparently thought otherwise.

'Why wait one more day, one more hour to heal this man?' he demanded. 'Why should he have one less moment of his life to be whole and healthy? Why not give him new life *now*?'

No-one answered. Not one of us had the courage to say what I was beginning to think: that it is right – and *necessary* – to do good now. To help and to heal *now*. Not to wait for the convenience of the end of Sabbath. We waited in silence – and we all knew what Jesus would do.

'Stretch out your hand', he said to the the man in front of him.

He stretched it out and as we watched, the limp fingers straightened, the wrinkled skin grew smooth and the muscles of wrist and hand grew firm and strong. The man began to laugh as he curled his fingers and and flexed his once useless hand, turning it this way and that, clasping an imaginary tool. His joy was wondrous to see.

I felt the disapproval of my fellow members of the Sanhedrin. I knew what they were thinking: another breach of the Sabbath; this man is dangerous; something must be done about him. But I found my thoughts running counter to theirs.

All I could think was: that it is right to do good – *here and now*.

***

Deathly sleep

Mark 5: 21 – 24, 35 – 43

'My little daughter is very ill, please come and place your hands on her …'

We were not too concerned at first, my wife and I. Our little daughter, standing on the threshold of womanhood had begun to lose some of her childish liveliness. She had always been a quick, impulsive child, running to meet me when I came home from synagogue duties, dancing, laughing, full of life and fun. But coming up to her twelfth birthday, she grew quieter. We thought it was all part of the business of growing up. My wife said, laughing, perhaps she will now become a little more *dignified* in her behaviour!

But it was not just growing up. She became pale, listless, complained of pain in her arms and legs. I called in a physician, who prescribed a little wine mixed with myrrh to relieve her pain and then instructed my wife to anoint the child's body with oil mixed with cinnamon. Neither remedy seemed to do her any good, and in desperation my wife insisted I find the man, Jesus. He was known to be a healer; he could heal our daughter, she insisted.

I was appalled! This man was a heretic, with dangerous ideas which went totally against our established laws, one to whom the doors of our synagogue were firmly closed under the orders of the priests. How could I, responsible for the good management of the synagogue, go to him and ask him to heal our child? But my wife was insistent. If I did not go and find him, she said, our precious daughter would die.

I set aside my dignity and my pride and went and found this man Jesus. He was half a days' journey away, but at my request he consented to come back with me. I was full of anxiety that we would be too late, and felt exasperated that he stopped to talk with a woman who had jostled him in the crowd. Especially when I saw messengers from my household hurrying to meet us. They came with the very worst of news.

She was dead, my lovely little daughter was dead. It was too late.

My servants said we should not trouble the teacher any more. Indeed I also thought there was now no point in asking Jesus to come back with me. To my surprise, he disagreed and said he would come to the house. He told me not to be afraid, simply believe.

Believe what? What did he think he could do now, except mourn with us? Join with the wailing women whose cries we could already hear? The funeral customs had already begun. Jesus dismissed all that.

'What are you making all this noise about? Why so distressed? The child is asleep.'

Mocking laughter mixed with the noise of weeping, the frantic wailing, the tearing of hair and garments. But Jesus remained calm and quiet. He went into the house with just myself, my wife and three of his friends. Our child was lying still and white, not a breath stirred her. What could he do for her now, healer though he was said to be?

He looked at her for a minute, then took hold of her limp hand.

'Talitha cumi' he said softly, 'little one, you can get up'.

She stirred, drew a deep breath, blinked and looked up at him. Then she sat up, and I saw through my tears the colour begin to come back to her face. She smiled as she looked round at us, then slowly got up, took a few faltering steps, then ran to her mother, and then to me.

Jesus told us not to spread this about.

'Tell no-one', he said. And he added:

'I think she might be hungry!'

It was hardly believable. My servants could not say a word. I took my girl's hand and went to show her to the crowd who had come to mourn her death.

The noise of weeping and wailing died away.

The whole crowd became completely silent, and in silence, melted away.

We were left together, my daughter and me.

***

Secret problem

Mark 5: 25 – 34

'There was a woman who had suffered from severe bleeding…'

For most women, when they reach the age of maturity, there comes the small time each month when they are most aware of their womanhood. A flow of blood, lasting perhaps only a few days, when we know we need to keep apart, knowing the Law considers us unclean for this short time. For most women, this is understood to be all part of being what we are, what we can do: to bear children; to carry out our part in God's great creation.

But for some of us it is not so. For a few of us, the time of our uncleanness lasts more than a few days, lasts for most of the month. I was one of the few. For the past twelve years I had to keep apart, aware of my uncleanness, aware of the pain and the mess, of the almost constant flow of blood. I could not go to the synagogue; I could go to the market only when it was closing and there were few others to come near me. I could not meet at the well and gossip with friends.

I had tried all the tonics and medicines set out in the Talmud; I had even tried magic potions, and so-called cures, such as wrapping the ashes of an ostrich egg in linen or cotton and carrying it with me everywhere. I had washed my face and hands in early morning dew; I had tried many various ointments rubbed over my body; I had drunk water mixed with mint and hyssop. Nothing helped.

I heard of the healer and preacher Jesus of Nazareth. But how could I go to him and tell of this woman's thing which I suffered? How could I ask him to heal me without telling him of my problem? There was always a crowd round him of his friends and disciples – how could I explain womanly things in front of them – a group of men?

But then I thought: perhaps being in a crowd might be of help. I could creep up quietly behind him and perhaps just touch his robe. I felt sure that alone would help me. But even that was not an easy thing to do. I went to the edge of the crowd who had gathered and were listening as he told stories as he walked along. I managed to come up behind Jesus just close enough to touch the tassel on his robe. And then slipped away as quickly as I could.

Suddenly I felt well! I felt the dragging pain ebb away. I knew I was no longer oozing blood. I felt clean, whole, proper woman.

But then things went wrong. Jesus had stopped, turned round, was looking at the people crowding round him. His voice came clear and loud:

'Who touched me?'

There were lots of people crowding him. Even his disciples were asking him what he meant. What did he mean? Did he know it was not just a touch but something more, something different, something to do with – me?

I was very afraid. What had I done? Would he take back the healing if I went and told him? He kept looking round to see who had touched him, not just a jostle from the crowd, but a touch with intent. I had to tell what I had done.

The crowd parted to let me through. I knelt down and began, shyly, hesitantly to tell him of my trouble. Once started, I could not stop, but poured it all out: the years of pain, feelings of disgrace, uncleanness, humiliation. I told him the whole sorry truth.

He listened quietly, as though he understood everything. And I began to understand something of what it cost him to allow me to be healed. It's not easy to explain.

He raised me to my feet and we stood together: the healer and the healed, and the pain which had ebbed away from me was marked on his face. But then, he smiled.

'Daughter', he said, 'it was your faith which brought you to me. Go in peace; you are healed of your trouble.'

The crowd moved on, sweeping past me as I stood by the road.

I had a new clean body, a new life to live, a new purpose for each day.

I could meet and talk with other women, with people in the synagogue.

I could now tell everyone what Jesus the healer had done for me.

***

A foreigner's faith

Mark 7: 24 – 30

> *'Jesus .. went away to the territory near the city of Tyre .. A woman, whose daughter had an evil spirit in her, heard about Jesus and came to him at once and fell at his feet. The woman was a Gentile, born in the region of Phoenicia in Syria. She begged Jesus to drive the demon out of her daughter.'*

What on this good earth made me think he would listen to me? Even more, that he would give me what I asked for – to restore my poor daughter to health? Since her early days she would have strange fits; she would shake and shiver, moaning odd sounds that were not words. Then, suddenly she would cry out loud and flap her hands about her head, as though she was trying to shake off an insect that was bothering her. Other times she would be quite silent, not answering any word spoken to her as though she were quite deaf. She could not talk properly, could not feed herself, would sit and rock to and fro, would not look at anyone, not even me, her mother.

I'd heard about him – this man Jesus. Women's gossip from the market place or from meetings at the well. These had brought news of this strange Jewish teacher and healer. Remarkable tales were told of what he had done: cured a leper, restored a damaged hand, woken a girl from death – well, almost death – so the stories went. But he was a Jew and the Jews don't like us Phoenicians. Any more than we like them. But that's the political bit, and all goes back to when Israel invaded our land – oh, thousands of years ago – and one of their tribes was *given* our country – by their God.

So they say.

Well, what would I know about that? We stick to our own gods and let them have their One and Only. That's up to them. I know they – the Jews – won't have anything to do with us, so why was this Jewish teacher here? What was he doing here? There were no answers to that and anyway, what did it matter? He was here, and I could go and see him, tell him that all I wanted was my little girl restored to the happy, healthy child she ought to be. And that I was desperate enough to go to a Jewish healer to get it!

I found him in the house of Ittai, a Jewish sympathiser. Someone pointed him out to me and I went straight up to him and knelt at his feet. Came straight out with my request – I thought if I didn't ask at once I'd lose what little courage I had.

'Please,' I said, 'I know you are a great healer. Will you cast the evil demon out of my daughter?'

He didn't reply. So I begged again. And again. The men round him told him to get rid of me.

He looked at me, and his look was kindly. Twinkling. As though he was pretending to be annoyed – and yet somehow wasn't. Can't explain it better than that. Then he said:

'The children have to be fed first, I can't take their food and give it to the puppy-dogs.'

'No,' I said instantly, 'but the puppies can eat the bits the children throw away!'

He laughed!

'A good answer! For that, and for your faith, go on your way. You will find the demon has gone out of your daughter.'

Was that it? Just go away and I would find things better? But how soon? And how much better? Did I really believe that? I got up, and went away. I didn't hurry. My mother was minding my child. I had a feeling that if I went slowly home, the healing – if that was what it was – would have time to work. Yes, I know that sounds silly but I really think now that I doubted the power of the man. I did not want to get home and find things were just as they had been and no better.

As I approached home, mother came to meet me. She was excited, could hardly get the words out.

'Amazing! Wonderful!' she babbled. 'A miracle. Come and see. Come quick!'

She almost dragged me into the house.

'About an hour ago,' she said, 'she was crying out and shaking all over, as bad as I've ever known her. Then suddenly she went quiet, but not her usual sort of quiet where she rocks and rocks and doesn't look at anyone. She looked up at me and smiled, as though she knew me! Then she turned over and went to sleep – a lovely, gentle sleep. The demon has gone. Come and see!'

***

Speech Therapy

Mark 7: 31 – 37

'Some people brought him a man who was deaf and could hardly speak ...'

'Can't hear, can't speak.'

'Deaf and daft.'

'Babbles like a baby.'

They thought because I could not hear them I did not know what they were saying about me. Back in the time of my deafness, they thought they could say what they liked and I wouldn't know.

To some extent they were right: I did not *know,* but I could interpret the looks, the mockery, the laughter. I could not hear my own voice, or how the words I was trying to say came out. I did not know how the words should sound when people spoke to me; I could only watch their mouths and try to make the same shapes.

Sometimes it was good to give up trying, to retreat into my world of almost-silence, to watch the play of light on the water of Lake Galilee, and the movement of the little boats. It was good to notice the smells of the fish as I helped haul the boats up from the water and see the shimmer-silver of their wriggling bodies as the nets were emptied of their catch. I helped with mending the nets, being good at using my hands. There were other smells too: up on the hills I caught the scent of the white flowers of the myrtle bushes, pine wood and cedar, and herbs growing wild. But it was not until after my healing that I learned the names of them, and learned to give thanks to God for them.

But I have not told you of my healing.

Although there were those who mocked and laughed at me, there were others who tried to help and befriend me, and it was these good folk who brought me to the healer. I was puzzled and a bit fearful; crowds confuse and upset me, there is too much activity and I did not understand what they were telling him; I did not understand what they wanted me to do. I looked from one to another, trying to see what was happening. The crowd were pushing in, watching, wanting to see what would happen.

But then he, the healer, gently took my arm and led me away. Away from the crowd. He began to make signs to me to help me understand what was happening. This I knew, I could understand. My parents had often signed: pointing to things, showing me what to do.

The healer touched my ears, then he spat on his fingers and put them to my ears. He breathed a deep sigh, and I felt the warmth of his breath. He moved my mouth and touched my tongue. I saw his lips move and I felt that he understood my problems with hearing and speaking. He then looked up into the sky, the blue of the heaven, the place where God was, and I saw he said something – a word.

But it was a word of power, of opening, of curing. I felt my ears pop, open. I heard sounds rush in as though a door had opened; a door which had shut out the sounds of the world and now let them all in with a babble of confusion and noise. I watched his lips – something I had always done to try and understand what was being said to me – and I heard him say clearly:

'Go in peace. You are healed.'

At first, I could not sort out the world of sound. I could not recognise the noise of the wind, of the waves, of the footsteps of people, of the sound of voices, of the meaning of words. So I did what I had always done: watched carefully and began to fit sound with sight.

It was a new and joyous experience! I learned the names of things, actions, smells, and began to fit them together. I listened to my own voice repeating what others said, finding with amazement I could say words clearly enough to be understood.

The mocking laughter was gone.

Now people laughed with me, named things for me, told me stories.

Now I could speak, and be understood.

Now I could tell the world my own story.

***

Blind Cure

Mark 8: 22 – 26

… some people brought a blind man to Jesus and begged him to touch him.

Where do I begin? From the beginning, when I could see with the eyes of childhood, but did not know that my early seeing was not as others saw? From the time when what I now understand to be the softening and blurring of my world began? From when the darkness edged in and narrowed my vision to a centre-point of faint light? Looking back, I can trace my blindness through its growing and spreading across my world, my life.

I had memories of early sight: my mother would sit me under the almond tree and watch as I stretched my hands out to try and catch the leaves waving above my head. She told me later of how she worried when I would screw up my eyes, would gaze intently at some small thing I had found: a stone, a leaf, a flower. She worried more when I would stumble and fall over something I should have seen – and did not. Or when I would stare at people walking towards us and not know till they came close that they were people I knew: my brothers, my father, my mother's sister.

When it was time for me to go to synagogue school, it was our Rabbi who told my mother gently what she had suspected – that I was nearly completely blind.

So I had become blind. But there were things I could do. I could work with my hands. As my sight grew less, so my sense of touch grew stronger. My father was a potter and I went to work with him in the workshop. At first he would only let me puddle the clay, trampling the raw material, carefully mixed with water, so that it made a fine smooth clay with no air pockets, easy to work with. Later, I was allowed to mould a few pots by hand, using rough thick clay which my father would later shape on the wheel. But soon, my father realised I had a gentle touch and could model well-shaped pots. So then I learned how to use the wheel. Soon I could model lamps, pitchers and bowls which, I was

told, fetched good prices in the market. But I could not see well enough to decorate or paint my work, which was something I longed to be able to do. At least I was useful, but there were times when I wanted to be more than just useful. To be able to make beautiful objects from the start of the potting process to its final completion. Was that too much to ask?

Later, I wanted to tell the healer what I had been able to do, thanks to his amazing power. What I remember most of that day was *kindness* – the kindness of those who told me of the man Jesus, and the wonderful things he had done for others; who brought me to him, who asked him to help me. Most of all, the kindness of the man himself. He took me by the hand and led me out of the village, away from the crowd. He spat on his hands and smeared it on my eyes.

'What can you see?' he asked.

I looked around. I saw the trees of my childhood place, but they were moving. I remembered as a small child, peering at people walking, and thinking they were the trees. It seemed the same now.

'Trees,' I said. 'Trees, like people. Walking trees.'

'Close your eyes', he said, so I did. I felt his hands on my face again, smoothing away the crusty skin round my eyes.

'What can you see now?'

I stared. It was his face I saw first.

His eyes, looking at me. His brows, raised, questioning.

'I can see – you,' I said. 'And I can see the hills. And grass, flowers. And people. The white road into the village. Blue sky. I can see my hands. I can *see!*'

He laughed then.

'Go then in faith,' he said, 'but not into the village yet. You need to learn to make your way in a seeing world, without a crowd round you. You need to find your own steps into your own place. Go in peace'.

Back in my workshop I began a new life as a potter who could see his work. I resolved to make beautifully decorated pots, bowls, pitchers and jars for oil or wine, and to make them for use in the synagogue as well as for the market place. I wanted my work to be the best it could be.

In gratitude to the healer.

***

Despair to hope

Mark 9: 14 – 24

'Teacher, I brought my son to you because he has an evil spirit in him ...'

We were in the middle of an argument and for once, my boy Joel was quiet. Usually any noise of upraised voices sets off the evil spirit in him, which shouts and screams and sends Joel shaking and spitting, often then throwing him to the ground. But when he is quiet, he is in his own world, which seems not to belong to our world.

I had brought him to see the teacher, Jesus-bar-Joseph of Nazareth. I was told he could help my boy, perhaps drive out the bad spirit, set him free. But he was not there, although a group of men who said they were his disciples were talking with people in the crowd. So I asked them to heal my son.

It seemed the obvious thing to do, but what a fuss it caused!

They said they could try. They were kindly and obviously wanted to help but had no idea how their master had done his healing. They put their hands on the boy, which made him shiver and cry out; they said some words of scripture, and called to the spirit to 'Come out!' But nothing happened except that Joel continued to shake uncontrollably. Some scribes and lawyers began to protest:

'These men can do nothing! Why do they think they can carry out an act of healing? Who do they think they are? Nothing but charlatans, just like their master!'

Some of the crowd started to argue, as did the group of disciples. I led my son away, the noise was upsetting him.

Then suddenly the man Jesus was with us. Just when we needed him most – he was there. Everyone was surprised, and the disciples were relieved to see him. He picked up on the situation at once.

'What's all the fuss and argument about?' he asked.

I was embarrassed.

'It's my fault, sir,' I said. 'I brought my son to you because he has a spirit which attacks him. It makes him unable to talk, throws him on the ground and he foams at the mouth. He grinds his teeth and goes rigid. I asked your disciples to cast the spirit out of him, and they tried but could not do it.'

He looked at me and at the disciples, and his look was a mixture of sadness and exasperation.

'What a hopeless lot you are! How long will it be before you understand? How much longer must I put up with you? Bring the boy here.'

We brought Joel, who came, dragging his feet, looking frightened. As soon as he saw Jesus, the devil in him seemed to wake and he went into as bad a fit as I have ever seen in him.

'How long has the poor child been like this?' he asked.

'Ever since he was a very small boy. The spirit seems to have tried to kill him at times; throwing him into the fire or into the lake. Please, help us. If you can'.

'I can,' he said, 'and I will. But you must believe I can.'

'I do believe,' I cried out at once. 'Help me believe better!'

I hardly knew what I was saying – only that it seemed important to say it. Jesus turned to my son and spoke firmly:

'Deaf and dumb spirit, hear me! Come out of this boy! Leave him, now!'

Joel screamed once, then fell to the ground, silent and very still. He looked as though he was dead. Indeed several people said he must be dead. I was very afraid. But Jesus stooped and took Joel by the hand.

'Up you get, my son,' he said. 'You have a new life to live'.

We both had a new life to live. Joel and I walked through the crowd together, quietly. He didn't stumble or shiver, but walked tall and straight.

'Wait till your mother sees you,' I said softly. He just grinned at me, a proper boyish grin, and gladness filled my heart.

I heard Jesus talking to his disciples, who wanted to know why they had been unable to drive the demon out.

'Faith,' I heard him say. 'Strong faith and prayer. Nothing else will do.'

***

Shout aloud

Mark 10: 46 – 52

… a blind beggar named Bartimaeus … was sitting by the road …'

We all knew Bartimaeus, blind Barty, loud-mouthed Barty. Sat at the northern gate on the road out of Jericho for years. Used to shout and curse at times, so much so that women were afraid of him. Not that he'd do them, or any one, any harm; it was just his anger at what he had become.

Because he hadn't always been blind. Looking back, we could see that it was not his fault.

What had his life been?

Jericho was a beautiful city, full of date and palm trees, rose gardens and groves of balsam which gave it the name of the perfumed city. But, as in every city, it had its poorer parts. Bartimaeus lived with his family in one of the very poorest parts of Jericho. His father was often drunk, his mother a poor thing who did her best but was worn out with struggling against life. Barty was a thin, dirty child, often to be seen playing in the street in the mud and rubbish, collecting bits and pieces of old pots to play with, broken bricks, sticks and stones.

As he grew older, those of us who knew him would shake out heads over his wild ways. He'd drink too much and get into fights; he didn't wash; tramped the hills in all weathers; didn't care where his food came from; probably knew too many women who were themselves no better than they should be. It was not surprising that his skin was often encrusted with sores, especially round the eyes, and perhaps inevitable that this would lead to blindness.

And anger and curses.

And wheedling for money, for all he could do in his blindness and poverty was beg.

On the day which was to change his life, Barty was in his usual place, whining for any pieces of money folk could spare. There was a crowd gathering, for people had heard that the preacher and healer Jesus was passing through Jericho on his way to Jerusalem. So they clustered round him to hear what he was saying as he went along. Barty wanted to know – as usual – what was going on, and when he heard Jesus of Nazareth was coming, he set up such a screech and a shout:

'Jesus, son of David, take pity on me!'

Everyone around told him to shut up; they wanted to hear what Jesus was saying. But he only shouted louder, and as we all knew he had a powerful voice! The more we tried to shut him up, the louder he shouted!

Jesus stopped. Stopped what he was saying, stopped in his tracks, asked to see whoever it was who was calling for help. So we hoisted Barty up and led him to Jesus.

'What do you want from me?' Jesus asked.

'My sight back,' said Barty promptly. 'I want to see again'.

He asked with all the certainty in his mind that Jesus could do this, could give him his sight.

Which he did.

'Go on your way,' Jesus said to Barty, 'it is your own faith which has given you your sight'.

The crowd moved on, carrying Jesus and his disciples with it. Barty stood by the wayside just staring round him. At the stones in the road; the people going by, who smiled at him, patted him on the back, laughed with him. At the trees, the sky. At the figure of Jesus, moving away down the road to Jerusalem. Finally, at himself.

If you met Bartimaeus now, you would not know him for the same blind, dirty beggar who sat by the road from Jericho to Jerusalem.

He cleaned up, sorted his life out, followed Jesus to the end.

He was there, silent and angry, on the day the crowd called for Jesus to be crucified.

He was there, near the cross, when they crucified him.

He was in Jerusalem when he heard the astonishing news of Jesus alive again– and believed it.

He was there with all those who gathered together in faith and joy, on the day we call Pentecost.

***

www.ingramcontent.com/pod-product-compliance
Lightning Source LLC
Chambersburg PA
CBHW071544080526
44588CB00011B/1794